How to Pray for Others One on One

Building Your Confidence to Use the Word in Your Prayers

PENNY RIDDLE

26 25 24 23 22   8 7 6 5 4 3 2 1

How to pray for others one on one
Copyright ©2022 Penny Riddle

All Rights Reserved. Except as permitted under the U.S. Copyright Act of 1976, no part of this publication may be reproduced, distributed, or transmitted in any form by any means, or stored in a database or retrieval system, without the prior written permission of the author and/or publisher.

Published by:
Barefoot Publishing

www.publishbarefoot.com

Library of Congress Cataloging-in-Publication Data:
ISBN: 978-1-0879-6035-7

Printed in the United States

A Note from the Author

For many years I have ministered the Word of God. I was once a phone minister at a church we attended and at that time, I did not know what scriptures to use when we were ministering to people over the phone or one on one. Thankfully, they provided us with manuals to use, so we would know what scriptures to encourage the people with.

I feel it is vital for all born again Christians to know what scriptures to use and not only that but know how to pray the Word over the people. You see, it is so important for you as believers to know how to minister to your friends, loved ones and anyone you come in contact with. Your pastors are not always going to be there, so it is very important for you to know how to lead someone to Jesus and not feel uncomfortable because you don't know where the scriptures are or what to pray for that certain thing. I pray this will be an instrument that will help you flow in all that God has for you.

Salvation

Below are the scriptures to share with someone who is in need of salvation:

Romans 10:8-10 (KJV)

⁸ But what saith it? The word is nigh thee, even in thy mouth, and in thy heart: that is, the word of faith, which we preach;

⁹ That if thou shalt confess with thy mouth the Lord Jesus, and shalt believe in thine heart that

God hath raised him from the dead, thou shalt be saved.

[10] For with the heart man believeth unto righteousness; and with the mouth confession is made unto salvation.

Acts 4:12 (KJV)

[12] Neither is there salvation in any other: for there is none other name under heaven given among men, whereby we must be saved.

Mark 1:4 King James Version (KJV)

⁴ John did baptize in the wilderness, and preach the baptism of repentance for the remission of sins.

Luke 3:3 (KJV)

³ And he came into all the country about Jordan, preaching the baptism of repentance for the remission of sins;

Romans 11:29 (KJV)

²⁹ For the gifts and calling of God are without repentance.

2 Peter 3:9 (KJV)

The Lord is not slack concerning his promise, as some men count slackness; but is longsuffering to us-ward, not willing that any should perish, but that all should come to repentance.

After you share the scriptures, here is the prayer to pray with someone needing salvation. Tell them to "repeat after me."

Salvation prayer

> Lord Jesus, I ask you right now, to forgive me from all my sins - past, present and future. I believe you died on the cross and rose again. Come into my heart. In Jesus name, amen.

I know what you are thinking, *this is such a short and simple prayer.* You're right!

It is simple. People are what make it hard and difficult. Remember, Jesus does not make things hard, we do. He is there to hear your simple prayer and He will answer you. That is the thing I love about our Lord Jesus Christ.

Baptism in the Holy Spirit

When you are ministering to someone to receive their prayer language, you pray with them just like you do for salvation. But instead of them repeating the sinner's prayer, you have them repeat this, *Lord you said in Your Word that if I ask for the baptism of the Holy Spirit with the evidence of speaking in tongues that You would give it to me. So, I am asking you right now in the name of Jesus for my heavenly prayer language with the evidence of speaking in tongues; right now, in Jesus name, amen.*

Then, just begin to start praying in the Holy Ghost and He will fill them. Make sure they know that God is not going to grab their tongue or mouth for them. They have to use their mouth by opening up their mouth and start speaking. Make sure they know that it is just like a baby when they are learning how to talk. They are not speaking in words yet, they are saying syllables. That is exactly what we do when we are praying in the spirit. Make sure they also know that the Word says they are praying mysteries- the perfect prayer- and that is why the devil does not what us to learn about the baptism of the Holy Spirit or wants us to receive our prayer language because he cannot understand it.

Your prayer language is a direct line to the Father and it is the most important gift you can receive from the Lord. The cool thing is, that it is a free gift that Jesus wants all the believers to have. When you first start praying in the Holy Spirit, (you will think I am making this up but trust me) even if you get one syllable, keep speaking it and I promise if you do that every day it will increase. You see, the devil and people will try to talk you out of this by saying this is not of God and that it is of the devil. Well, let me assure you if it was of the devil, everyone in the world would be doing it because they do everything else the devil has to offer.

So here are the scriptures to give to the people and a prayer at the end:

Luke 11:13

¹³ If you then, being evil, know how to give good gifts to your children, how much more will your heavenly Father give the Holy Spirit to those who ask Him!"

Acts 2:1-4

² When the Day of Pentecost had fully come, they were all with one accord[a] in one place. ² And suddenly there came a sound from heaven, as of a rushing mighty wind, and it filled the whole house where they were sitting. ³ Then there appeared to them divided tongues, as of fire, and one sat upon each of them. ⁴ And they were all filled with the Holy Spirit and began to speak with other tongues, as the Spirit gave them utterance.

Matthew 3:11 (KJV)

¹¹ I indeed baptize you with water unto repentance. but he that cometh after me is mightier than I, whose shoes I am not worthy to bear: he shall baptize you with the Holy Ghost, and with fire:

Luke 1:35 (KJV)

³⁵ And the angel answered and said unto her, The Holy Ghost shall come upon thee, and the power of the Highest shall overshadow thee: therefore also that holy thing which shall be born of thee shall be called the Son of God.

John 14:26 (KJV)

²⁶ But the Comforter, which is the Holy Ghost, whom the Father will send in my name, he shall teach you all things, and bring all things to your remembrance, whatsoever I have said unto you.

John 20:22 (KJV)

²² And when he had said this, he breathed on them, and saith unto them, Receive ye the Holy Ghost:

Acts 1:8 (KJV)

⁸ But ye shall receive power, after that the Holy Ghost is come upon you: and ye shall be witnesses unto me both in Jerusalem, and in all Judaea, and in Samaria, and unto the uttermost part of the earth.

Acts 2:38 (KJV)

³⁸ Then Peter said unto them, Repent, and be baptized every one of you in the name of Jesus Christ for the remission of sins, and ye shall receive the gift of the Holy Ghost.

Acts 4:31 (KJV)

³¹ And when they had prayed, the place was shaken where they were assembled together; and they were all filled with the Holy Ghost, and they spake the word of God with boldness.

Acts 8:17 (KJV)

17 Then laid they their hands on them, and they received the Holy Ghost.

Acts 13:52 (KJV)

52 And the disciples were filled with joy, and with the Holy Ghost.

Acts 19:2 (KJV)

2 He said unto them, Have ye received the Holy Ghost since ye believed? And they said unto him, We have not so much as heard whether there be any Holy Ghost.

Acts 19:6 (KJV)

⁶ And when Paul had laid his hands upon them, the Holy Ghost came on them; and they spake with tongues, and prophesied.

Jude 20 (KJV)

²⁰ But ye, beloved, building up yourselves on your most

holy faith, praying in the Holy Ghost,

1 Corinthians 14:18 (KJV)

¹⁸ I thank my God, I speak with tongues more than ye all:

1 Corinthians 14:2 (KJV)

² For he that speaketh in an unknown tongue speaketh not unto men, but unto God: for no man understandeth him; howbeit in the spirit he speaketh mysteries.

Let them know that the Lord is not going to come down and make them speak in tongues. Tell them that you receive your prayer language by faith, and then when they get through repeating the prayer with you, that you are going to start praying in the Spirit and that they can receive at that time. They need to open their mouth and start speaking it out. You can share with them that sometimes it comes in one syllable, and sometimes more, but use the first word that the Lord gives you and then you will see that it grows as you keep praying. So, every day it will become more and more.

Prayer

Now lay your hands on them and have them repeat this prayer after you:

Heavenly Father you said in your word that if anyone asks for the baptism of the Holy Spirit they could have it, so I am asking you right now to fill me with the Holy Spirit with the evidence of speaking in tongues and I believe and I receive it now by faith in Jesus name.

Now, start praying in the Spirit and God will show up and fill them.

Scriptures for your Physical Ailments

Psalms 103:1-5

Bless the LORD, O my soul; And all that is within me, bless His holy name!

Bless the LORD, O my soul, And forget not all His benefits: Psalms 103:3 Who forgives all your iniquities, Who heals all your diseases, Psalms 103:4 Who redeems your life from destruction,

*Who crowns you with loving
kindness and tender mercies,*

*Who satisfies your mouth with good things,
So that your youth is renewed like the eagle*

3 John 1: 2

*Beloved, I pray that you may prosper in all things
and be in health, just as your soul prospers.*

Isaiah 40: 31

*But those who wait on the LORD Shall
renew their strength; They shall mount up
with wings like eagles, They shall run and not
be weary, They shall walk and not faint.*

Galatians 3:13

Christ has redeemed us from the curse of the law, having become a curse for us (for it is written, Cursed is everyone who hangs on a tree;),

Galatians 3:14

that the blessing of Abraham might come upon the Gentiles in Christ Jesus, that we might receive the promise of the Spirit through faith.

Psalms 91:9-11

Because you have made the LORD, who is my refuge, Even the Most High, your dwelling place, No evil shall befall you, Nor shall any plague come near your dwelling;

For He shall give His angels charge over you, To keep you in all your ways.

Exodus 15:26 (AMP)

saying, "If you will diligently listen and pay attention to the voice of the LORD your God, and do what is right in His sight, and listen to His commandments, and keep [foremost in your thoughts and actively obey] all His precepts and statutes, then I will not put on you any of the diseases which I have put on the Egyptians; for I am the [a]LORD who heals you."

Exodus 23:25 (KJV)

And ye shall serve the LORD your God, and he shall bless thy bread, and thy water; and I will take sickness away from the midst of thee.

1 Peter 2:24

who Himself bore our sins in His own body on the tree, that we, having died to sins, might live for righteousness— by whose stripes you were healed.

Isaiah 58:8

Then your light shall break forth like the morning, Your healing shall spring forth speedily, And your righteousness shall go before you; The glory of the LORD shall be your rear guard.

Matthew 4:23

[Jesus Heals a Great Multitude] And Jesus went about all Galilee, teaching in their synagogues, preaching the gospel of the kingdom, and healing all kinds of sickness and all kinds of disease among the people.

Matthew 9:35

[*The Compassion of Jesus*] Then Jesus went about all the cities and villages, teaching in their synagogues, preaching the gospel of the kingdom, and healing every sickness and every disease among the people.

Luke 9:11

But when the multitudes knew it, they followed Him; and He received them and spoke to them about the kingdom of God, and healed those who had need of healing.

Acts 10:38

how God anointed Jesus of Nazareth with the Holy Spirit and with power, who went about doing good and healing all who were oppressed by the devil, for God was with Him.

Isaiah 53:4-5 (KJV)

4 Surely he hath borne our griefs, and carried our sorrows: yet we did esteem him stricken, smitten of God, and afflicted.

5 But he was wounded for our transgressions, he was bruised for our iniquities: the chastisement of our peace was upon him; and with his stripes we are healed.

Prayer

Father we give you praise and honor today and thank you that by Jesus Stripes we are healed. We know and believe Lord Jesus that you according to Isaiah 53:4-5,

That you bore our grief and carried our sorrows, and we don't have to live in sorrow no more. We know You were wounded for our transgressions, and bruised for our iniquities the chastisement for our peace was upon You and by Your stripes we are healed. Lord Jesus we thank you today that we are living and walking in divine health and that no weapon formed against us will prosper.

Heavenly Father, we believe according to your word in 3 John 2 that you desire above all things that we prosper and be in health even as our souls prosper.

Thank you in the name of Jesus! Psalms 103:3, Who forgives all your iniquities, Who heals all your diseases, amen.

How to Minister Deliverance

Psalms 18:50

*Great **deliverance** He gives to His king, And shows mercy to His anointed, To David and his descendants forevermore.*

Psalms 32:7

*You are my hiding place; You shall preserve me from trouble; You shall surround me with songs of **deliverance**. Selah*

Philippians 1:19

*[To Live Is Christ] For I know that this will turn out for my **deliverance** through your prayer and the supply of the Spirit of Jesus Christ,*

Prayer

Father you said in your Word, in Psalms 18:50, that great **deliverance** you give to kings and to your descendants and you show mercy to your anointed and I am your descendant, and you also said in your Word that if we lay hands on the sick they shall recover. Now, we are laying hands on (name the person) right now and we are standing with them that they are healed from the top of their heads to the soles of their feet. You also said that in First Peter 2:24 by Jesus' stripes, they are healed. And you said if two or more agree on anything it shall be done by our father in heaven so we are in agreement that they are healed now right now! We curse every sickness and every disease everything they need

deliverance from off their body right now in Jesus name, Amen.

How to Pray for Someone with Addictions

If you are having problems with drugs or alcohol, food etc., this is for you!

Here is a little testimony from my husband, Pastor Rick Riddle. He had a problem with alcohol and drugs and more. When he got born again, he was instantly delivered from drugs and alcohol but he had the hardest time giving up cigarette's so he used this scripture, 1 Corinthians 10:13 (see below). I encourage you to read the whole chapter of I Corinthians 10.

This scripture helped him get totally free from that. Another thing that he has told people trying to give up their cigarettes, is to get your cigarette out and light it up and say, *"Lord I just want to praise you with this cigarette."* You cannot do it and that helps you to lay it down. Get the Scripture in your heart. Learn it, memorize it, and every time you feel that temptation come, quote this Scripture. The Word never fails!

Corinthians 10:13

No temptation has overtaken you except such as is common to man; but God is faithful, who will not allow you to be tempted beyond what you are able, but with the temptation will also make the way of escape, that you may be able to bear it.

Prayer

Father we thank you for healing (add their name). We know that you said in your Word that you sent your Word and healed us from any sickness or disease. We curse every addiction, every demonic force that is holding this precious person in bondage. We take authority over this addiction now and command it to leave in Jesus name. We plead the blood over them now. In Jesus name, amen.

Praying for Finances

Philippians 4:17-19

Not that I seek the gift, but I seek the fruit that abounds to your account.

Indeed I have all and abound. I am full, having received from Epaphroditus the things sent from you, a sweet-smelling aroma, an acceptable sacrifice, well pleasing to God. And my God shall supply all your need according to His riches in glory by Christ Jesus.

Malachi 3:10 -12

Bring all the tithes into the storehouse, That there may be food in My house, And try Me now in this Says the LORD of hosts, If I will not open for you the windows of heaven And pour out for you such blessing That there will not be room enough to receive it.

And I will rebuke the devourer for your sakes, So that he will not destroy the fruit of your ground, Nor shall the vine fail to bear fruit for you in the field Says the LORD of hosts;

And all nations will call you blessed, For you will be a delightful land, Says the LORD of hosts.

Deuteronomy 8:18

*And you shall remember the LORD your God,
for it is He who gives you power to get wealth,
that He may establish His covenant which
He swore to your fathers, as it is this day.*

Deuteronomy 28:1-13

*Now it shall come to pass, if you diligently obey
the voice of the LORD your God, to observe
carefully all His commandments which I
command you today, that the LORD your God
will set you high above all nations of the earth.*

*And all these blessings shall come upon
you and overtake you, because you obey
the voice of the LORD your God:*

*Blessed shall you be in the city, and
blessed shall you be in the country.*

*Blessed shall be the fruit of your body, the
produce of your ground and the increase
of your herds, the increase of your cattle
and the offspring of your flocks.*

*Blessed shall be your basket and
your kneading bowl.*

*Blessed shall you be when you come in, and
blessed shall you be when you go out.*

*The LORD will cause your enemies who
rise against you to be defeated before your
face; they shall come out against you one
way and flee before you seven ways.*

*The LORD will command the blessing on you
in your storehouses and in all to which you set
your hand, and He will bless you in the land
which the LORD your God is giving you.*

The LORD will establish you as a holy people to Himself, just as He has sworn to you, if you keep the commandments of the LORD your God and walk in His ways.

Then all peoples of the earth shall see that you are called by the name of the LORD, and they shall be afraid of you.

And the LORD will grant you plenty of goods, in the fruit of your body, in the increase of your livestock, and in the produce of your ground, in the land of which the treasure, the heavens, to give the rain to your land in its season, and to bless all the work of your hand. You shall lend to many nations, but you shall not borrow.

And the LORD will make you the head and not the tail; you shall be above only, and not be beneath, if you heed the commandments of the LORD your God, which I command you today, and are careful to observe them.

Prayer

Lord we come today into Your presence thanking you for Your goodness and mercy. We stand and believe today according to Your Word in Psalms 35:27 that you take pleasure in the prosperity of your servants. We thank you for the financial provision of our family members as they serve You. Lord, we believe as we tithe and give offerings that You have opened up the windows of Heaven and You are pouring us out blessings that we don't have room enough to receive them and also that you have rebuked the devourer for our sakes in Jesus name, amen.

Scriptures for Being Strong Spiritually

Ephesians 1:17-23

That the God of our Lord Jesus Christ, the Father of glory, may give to you the spirit of wisdom and revelation in the knowledge of Him,

The eyes of your understanding being enlightened; that you may know what is the hope of His calling, what are the riches of the glory of His inheritance in the saints.

*and what is the exceeding greatness of His
power toward us who believe, according
to the working of His mighty power.*

*which He worked in Christ when He raised
Him from the dead and seated Him at
His right hand in the heavenly places.*

*far above all principality and power
and might and dominion, and every
name that is named, not only in this age
but also in that which is to come.*

*And He put all things under His feet, and gave
Him to be head over all things to the church.*

*which is His body, the fullness of
Him who fills all in all.*

Ephesians 6:10-18

*Finally, my brethren, be strong in the
Lord and in the power of His might.*

*Put on the whole armor of God, that you may
be able to stand against the wiles of the devil.*

*For we do not wrestle against flesh and blood, but
against principalities, against powers, against the
rulers of the darkness of this age, against spiritual
hosts of wickedness in the heavenly places.*

*Therefore take up the whole armor of God,
that you may be able to withstand in the
evil day, and having done all, to stand.*

*Stand therefore, having girded your
waist with truth, having put on the
breastplate of righteousness.*

*and having shod your feet with the preparation
of the gospel of peace. Above all, taking the*

shield of faith with which you will be able to quench all the fiery darts of the wicked one.

And take the helmet of salvation, and the sword of the Spirit, which is the word of God.

Praying always with all prayer and supplication in the Spirit, being watchful to this end with all perseverance and supplication for all the saints--

Prayer

Heavenly Father, I thank You that my family is hearing and discerning Your voice today as you speak wisdom and revelation into our hearts. I thank you and believe the eyes of our understanding is enlightened and we know what is the hope of Your calling. We know you have given us power over all the power of the enemy and that nothing by any means will harm us in Jesus name, amen

Scriptures for Mental Strength

Romans 12:1-2

I beseech you therefore, brethren, by the mercies of God, that you present your bodies a living sacrifice, holy, acceptable to God, which is your reasonable service.

And do not be conformed to this world, but be transformed by the renewing of your mind, that you may prove what is that good and acceptable and perfect will of God.

Romans 8:6-9

For to be carnally minded is death, but to be spiritually minded is life and peace.

Because the carnal mind is enmity against God; for it is not subject to the law of God, nor indeed can be.

So then, those who are in the flesh cannot please God.

But you are not in the flesh but in the Spirit, if indeed the Spirit of God dwells in you. Now if anyone does not have the Spirit of Christ, he is not His.

2 Corinthians 10:3-4

For though we walk in the flesh, we do not war according to the flesh.

For the weapons of our warfare are not carnal but mighty in God for pulling down strongholds, casting down arguments and every high thing that exalts itself against the knowledge of God, bringing every thought into captivity to the obedience of Christ.

Isaiah 26:3

You will keep him in perfect peace, whose mind is stayed on You, Because he trusts in You. Trust in the Lord forever, for in Yah, the Lord, is everlasting strength.

Prayer

Father, we pray and believe today that you are moving supernaturally on the behalf of our family and friends. We bind every demonic force and ungodly thought that would come against the minds of our family. Heavenly Father, Your Word says in Matthew 18:18 that whatever we bind on earth will be bound in Heaven so we bind the enemy's strongholds and bring into captivity every thought to the obedience of Christ. We pray and believe that we have the mind of Christ according to I Cor. 2:16. Thank you Lord that we are not conformed to this world, but we are transformed by the renewing of our minds unto the Word of God and that we know and understand what your perfect will is for our lives. We receive from your Holy Spirit today in the mighty matchless name of Jesus, amen.

A Week of Praying for Others

Monday
Pray for Your Families Spiritually

Heavenly Father, I thank You that my family is hearing and discerning your voice today as you speak wisdom and revelation into our hearts. I thank You and believe the eyes of our understanding is enlightened and we know what is the hope of Your calling. We know You have given us power over all the power of the enemy and that nothing by any means will harm us in Jesus name, amen.

Scripture References

Ephesians 1:17-23

Ephesians 6:10-18

Tuesday-

Pray for Your Families Mentally

Father, we pray and believe today that You are moving supernaturally on the behalf of our family and friends. We bind every demonic force and ungodly thought that would come against the minds of our family. Heavenly Father your word says in Matthew 18:18 that whatever we bind on earth will be bound in Heaven we bind the enemy's strongholds and bring into captivity every thought to the obedience of Christ. We pray and believe that we have the mind of Christ according to I Corinthians 2:16. Thank you Lord that we are not conformed to this world, but we are transformed by the renewing of our minds unto the Word of God and that we know and understand what Your perfect will is for our lives. We receive from Your Holy Spirit today in the mighty matchless name of Jesus, amen.

Scripture References

Romans 12:1-2

2 Corinthians 10:2-5

Isaiah 26:3

Romans 8:6-9

Wednesday

Pray for Your Families Physically

Father, we give You praise and honor today and thank You that by Jesus' stripes we are healed. We know and believe Lord Jesus that You, according to Isaiah 53: 4-5 have borne our grief and carried our sorrows, and we don't have to live in sorrow no more. We know You were wounded for our transgressions, and bruised for our iniquities the chastisement for our peace was upon You and by Your stripes we are healed.

Lord Jesus, we thank You today that we are living and walking in divine health and that no weapon formed against us will prosper.

Heavenly Father, we believe according to Your Word in 3 John 2, that You desire above all things that we prosper and be in health even as our souls prosper. Thank You in the name of Jesus, amen.

Scripture References

Psalms 103:1-5

Isaiah 40:31

Galatians 3:13-14

Psalms 91: 9-11

2 John 1:2

Thursday

Pray for your Family's Finances

Lord, we come today into Your presence thanking You for Your goodness and mercy. We stand and believe today according to Your word in Psalms 35: 27 that you take pleasure in the prosperity of your servants. We thank You for the financial provision of our family members as they serve You. Lord, we believe as we tithe and give offerings that You have opened up the windows of Heaven and You are pouring us out blessings we don't have room enough to receive them, also that You have rebuked the devourer for our sakes in Jesus name, amen.

Scripture References

Philippians 4:15-19

Malachi 3:10

Deuteronomy 8:18

Deuteronomy 28:1-13

Also check out these additional scripture references:

Job 36:11	Joel 2:23-32
Psalms 1: 1-3	Haggai 2:6-9
Psalms 23: 1-6	Matt. 6:20-33
Psalms 34: 4-10	Luke 6:38
Psalms 75:6-7	Mark 10:29-30
Psalms 112: 1- 10	John 4:34-38
Psalms 115: 12-16	John 10:10
Proverbs 3: 9-10	Acts 3:19-21
Proverbs 4: 4-13	Acts 4:20-35
Proverbs 8: 17-21	Romans 8:31-32
Proverbs 10: 22-24	Romans 13:8
Proverbs 11: 23-28	I Cor.9:7-14
Proverbs 13: 22	II Cor.8:9
Proverbs 19: 14-17	II Cor. 9:6-12
Eccl. 11:1-6	Gal. 6:7-10
Isa.45:2-3	Gal.3:13-14 Gal. 4:1-7
Isa. 48:16-18	I Tim. 6:10- 19
Isa.55:1-13	Heb. 7:5-10
Isa.58:1-14	James 5:1-7
Isa. 60:1-5	I Peter 4:8-10.
Jeremiah 33:3	

Friday

Pray for Your Loved One's Salvation

Heavenly Father, we thank you today for the salvation of our family and friends. We bind the forces of the enemy who is trying to influence them and we command the scales and blinders to come off of their eyes and minds that they can see the light of the glorious Gospel of Jesus Christ. We thank You for sending angels, ministers and witnesses across the paths of our loved ones, people who they will receive the Word of God from and we call them into Your kingdom today in Jesus name, amen.

Scripture References

Luke 10:1-2

After these things the Lord appointed seventy others also, and sent them two by two before His face into every city and place where He Himself was about to go.

Then He said to them, The harvest truly is great, but the laborers are few; therefore pray the Lord of the harvest to send out laborers into His harvest.

John 4:34-37

Jesus said to them, My food is to do the will of Him who sent Me, and to finish His work. Do you not say, There are still four months and then comes the harvest? Behold, I say to you, lift up your eyes and look at the fields, for they are already white for harvest!

And he who reaps receives wages, and gathers fruit for eternal life, that both he who sows and he who reaps may rejoice together.

For in this the saying is true: One sows and another reaps. John 4:38 I sent you to reap that for which you have not labored; others have labored, and you have entered into their labors.

Peter 3:9

The Lord is not slack concerning His promise, as some count slackness, but is longsuffering toward us, not willing that any should perish but that all should come to repentance.

Isaiah 54:13-17

All your children shall be taught by the LORD, And great shall be the peace of your children. In righteousness you shall be established; You shall be far from oppression, for you shall not fear; And from terror, for it shall not come near you.

Indeed they shall surely assemble, but not because of Me. Whoever assembles against you shall fall for your sake. Behold, I have created the blacksmith Who blows the coals in the fire, Who brings forth an instrument for his work; And I have created the spoiler to destroy. No weapon formed against you shall prosper, And every tongue which rises against you in judgment You shall condemn. This is the heritage of the servants of the LORD, And their righteousness is from Me, Says the LORD.

Saturday

Pray for the Right Relationships

Lord, we thank You today for opening doors that need to be opened and closing doors that need to be closed. We know that You bring people into our lives when You want to bless us and that You bring people into our lives when You want us to bless them. We give You praise today for divine appointments and divine connections that Your angels are going before us to set up and prepare. Father, we give You glory for the relationships You have already ordained and brought into our lives. We pray that we will always love and speak blessing into their lives in Jesus name, amen.

Scripture References

1 Corinthians 12:12-20

For as the body is one and has many members, but all the members of that one body, being many, are one body, so also is Christ. For by one Spirit we were all baptized into one body-- whether Jews or Greeks, whether slaves or free-- and have all been made to drink into one Spirit. For in fact the body is not one member but many. If the foot should say, Because I am not a hand, I am not of the body, is it therefore not of the body? 1 And if the ear should say, Because I am not an eye, I am not of the body is it therefore not of the body?

If the whole body were an eye, where would be the hearing? If the whole were hearing, where would be the smelling? But now God has set the members, each one of them, in the body just as He pleased. And if they were all one member, where would the body be? But now indeed there are many members, yet one body.

1 Corinthians 13:4-9

Love suffers long and is kind; love does not envy; love does not parade itself, is not puffed up; does not behave rudely, does not seek its own, is not provoked, thinks no evil; does not rejoice in iniquity, but rejoices in the truth; bears all things, believes all things, hopes all things, endures all things. Love never fails. But whether there are prophecies, they will fail; whether there are tongues, they will cease; whether there is knowledge, it will vanish away. For we know in part and we prophesy in part.

Galatians 5:22-26

But the fruit of the Spirit is love, joy, peace, longsuffering, kindness, goodness, faithfulness, gentleness, self-control. Against such there is no law. And those who are Christ have crucified the flesh with its passions and desires. If we live in the Spirit, let us also walk in the Spirit. Let us not become conceited, provoking one another, envying one another.

Ephesians 4:29-32

Let no corrupt word proceed out of your mouth, but what is good for necessary edification, that it may impart grace to the hearers. And do not grieve the Holy Spirit of God, by whom you were sealed for the day of redemption.

*Let all bitterness, wrath, anger, clamor, and
evil speaking be put away from you, with
all malice. And be kind to one another,
tenderhearted, forgiving one another,
even as God in Christ forgave you.*

Matthew 18:18-19

*Assuredly, I say to you, whatever you bind on
earth will be bound in heaven, and whatever
you loose on earth will be loosed in heaven.
Again I say to you that if two of you agree on
earth concerning anything that they ask, it will
be done for them by My Father in heaven.*

James 5:16

Confess your trespasses to one another, and pray for one another, that you may be healed. The effective, fervent prayer of a righteous man avails much.

2 Corinthians 9:6

But this I say: He who sows sparingly will also reap sparingly, and he who sows bountifully will also reap bountifully.

Sunday Assignment

Please sow bountiful prayers
for your family every week
so that you may reap a
bountiful harvest in your life
and family.

www.ingramcontent.com/pod-product-compliance
Lightning Source LLC
LaVergne TN
LVHW011738060526
838200LV00051B/3224